the very best webook poetry

2009

Design: John Mitrione

WEbook, Inc.
307 Fifth Avenue, 7th Floor
New York, NY 10016
646.453.8575
www.WEbook.com

ISBN: 978-1-935003-08-3

Library of Congress Cataloging-in-Publication Data has been applied for.

Printed in the United States.

Contents

Part 1: we of were, we of weep

Part II: we of wellspring, we of weed

PART III: we of weapon, we of web

Part IV: we of welded, we of wealth

I.

we of were,
we of weep

Black holes

by Nicole Bailey

water grows stagnant
in the vase of your arrangement
rose petals on the table
fallen from such great heights.
your letters, your chair, all speak to your absence
the shadows closing in early night,
dead air and red wine.

echo your feet on spiral stairs
the hum of silence where once was your voice.
your lips imprinted on your coffee mug
lend secrets I don't want to hear.

cascade,
your abandonment reeks of design.
the way your laundry still hangs
haunting the clothes lines.
it makes me clumsy,
the solitude of natural light
falling all over your image
as I'm closing my eyes.
a silent telephone stands alone in your place
adopts your air of indifference,
and my vague hopes are wasted
as I plunge into night.

in the absence of body
these things speak of you

She wept

by Milton Ryan Watson

She wept at the sight
Of the coming dawn
She dried her eyes
She felt so alone
Her heart was empty
Her love was gone
She wept at the sight
Of the coming dawn.

She held her hands
In front of her eyes
She wanted the darkness
In which to hide
She felt an ache
In her heart and sighed
She held her hands
In front of her eyes

Her head hung low
Tears filled her eyes
When she remembered
All his lies
Her love was gone
She so despised
All his words
That were nothing but lies

She wept,
With the coming of the night
Though she wanted darkness
In which to hide
His love was nothing
But damnable lies
She wept,
With the coming of the night.

Our Mystic Connexion is Wrecking Me

by Glenn Jr. Marchand

Too often
Is the thought
Of what I cannot enjoy.

If my essence glints
In thy mind, make
Arrant that passage.

I see thee in my mental
Mecca. This kinetic
Connexion has become
An unattainable manna.

But a barren vision, is the
Death of our souls, yearning!
Aquatic in depth, our
Passion brings the sea to
Boil.

Shall Shadrach,
Meshach and Abednego
Tame this furnace of fire?
I flame. Where art the Magi?

Within my mind, thou art
The host of Midian! Unfriendly
And hostile upon my senses.

One of the deepest mourns
Upon earth, is that space in
No time where satiation is
But a voidness of light.

Is it the interracial union that
Would wreck us? Would
Our parents revise their will?

My mind is taut with madness.
I am Job misunderstanding life.
I am David plotting for Bathsheba.
I am Jesus deprived of love.
Play the
Mystagogue, my amore.
Become the demigod of my
Senses.

Maybe I am afflicted
With mythomania; but my Naiad,
I long for thee as the Israelites
For Yahweh.

I am Nebuchadnezzer,
Bewitched, clawing the dirt.
I am Elijah, hopeless, burden
Of the cave. I am Hosea,
Without thee as my harlot.
I have nothing to fiddle
Through as Rome burns.

What of Nirvana I have attained,
Is now but a vacant piece of
Spirit. Do you prize the triumph?
The crush of me!

I carry this
Old man of the sea; this garm
Gnawing into my sprit-flesh.
Have I gone astray!
Have I become enchanted by
Penelope? Lust of the Sanhedrin
Court! Possession of but one man!

Thou art a Philistine to me:
The first wife of Samson;
The Pauline thorn.

Dear God, how I yearn for the
Philosopher's womb. But
Unto my bleeding mind, she
Has become Phobos; the god
Of my dread, the source of
My alarm.

Shall I become a
Phoenix? Shall I again drink
Of the Pierian Spring?—given
Life to this withering rose;
For I am haunted by the plagues
Of Egypt; scatted fragments of
Me drift through the desert. In
Tongues of flame I curse thee.

Thou art a promised land forever
Sought; a rabbit hole unto
Eternity; dementia of my mind;
A red sea which refuses to
Part.

I thought thee the Rembrandt
Of my art; the rivers of Babylon
Without mourn; I thought we
Would complete the scriptures.

But instead, here I sit upon Robben
Island, intellectually romantic,
Quixotic over a goddess I can
Never touch.

How do I outwit fate?
How do I resurrect the
Archives of our mysticism?
How do I become the tenets of
Thy life?

I am but a fantast. Tell
Me I can love again. Tell me I
Have not loved in vain. Split me
And thereby paint away the darkness.
Turn us into the poesy of William
Blake.

The Suicide

by Michael Joseph Murphy

Scarlet ribbons,
Blood red ribbons,
Slipping, sliding, warming,
Still.

Painted smile,
On death-white throat,
Drip-drop-drip on hurried
Note.

"Can't go on,
Too great the cost;
She has gone - all is
Lost."

A Long Year

by m.w. polis

Imagine that you shoot me with a slow bullet
That takes an hour or more
To kill me in tedious agony.

Or stab me with a dull dull knife
All the live-long day
More painful than the bullet.

Or a month of agonizing poisons
Unintended, your actions
Always feel like these

And now you are saying goodbye forever
Can we move this along, please?
It promises to be a long year.

An Elegy of Yesterday, As You Became She To Me

by Kayzzaman

An elegy
For ecstasy
For you
As I call you
Her
Of myself - from
Yours and mine

And or *not*
From hers and mine
Metamorphosed -
Into frozen guilts
Of losing you
And I call you her
In warmth
Of yesterday's likeness
Gone, all gone
To fix you on me
As her - just her,
Not deadening her as
Likeness of you -

As
Yesterday lasted
No more, no less
Than
Decomposing feelings

Like harlequin
Of not laughter - at all
But as sharing and cropping
Mephistopheles' miniatures
To rob me of you
From being unpardonable
So unpardonable
As she - like a siren
Damages you
Like your swelling bosoms
Sagging
And dying dead
To lovesay
In the fifth leaf
Of yesterday
A doggerel of yesterday

Yesterday
It was - only yesterday
You were you
You became she to me
And she became -
An elegy of ecstasy
Only for me

And for you only
It is yesterday, all yesterday
Exiled in her as you
Of yesterday
To lovesay you and me...

A Note to my Father in Brighton

by Vicki F. Chavis

Wincing through Brighton in heels, dragging a
wrinkled map around
like a permanent question mark, I almost collide with
a curb to avoid a city bus

on crack. Hissing to a stop, it unleashes three crabby
travelers into the Sabbath
morning air, fidgety and bent like S-shaped cat tails
caught in the door,

desperate, perhaps, for their cafe latte at the corner
kiosk. A baby propped
half-assed in her pram glances back at me with your
eyes, your face; feigning

interest in strangers, preferring instead to follow the
lines in her tiny palm.
Anchored beyond the harbor wall, her bow listing
slightly to port, nods

a venerable queen among commoners, the
quintessential liberator on this
final cruise with you. In the polished gleam of her
teak deck and handrails,

her essence of deep-water reach, it's all I can do to let
go a flurry of ashes,
aghast, by the speed of your leaving.

I just wanted to let you know that your life here
wasn't imagined, wasn't an
errant wind, although it's true, we're barely tethered
to earth and balance so

bravely on this sharp, unmappable ridge that borders
the other side.
The headiness of your laughter, unbridled, as always,
bridging the distance,

becomes the mile marker leading me home.
Leave the lights on for me, will you, Daddy?

Grey

by m.w. polis

Another sheet of ashen grey
Is stretched across the sky today
The ropes of rain, from silver weave unravel
There's nothing I love more than rain
The way it strikes the windowpane
And makes the sounds of children's feet on gravel

That picture's all I have of you
When clouds of slate let the sun slip through
The only one we had of us together
The light was dancing on your hair
I thought that I was dreaming there
I was, and I still am, and will forever

There will come a time before too long
When my past goes dark and my future's done
And the fire in me is just a dying ember
And lost to me, that moment there
When the light was dancing on your hair
When the sun broke through the grey skies of
December

So there it hangs on my bare wall
The one we took back in the fall
That photo of the two of us together
The sun broke out from the leaden skies
But now I see there in your eyes
A sadness, I swear to God I don't remember

Indignation

by Nancy Jacobsen

I am
mismatched, misplaced;
smeared, wrung out and defaced.
Those hateful words I spat out,
Strangled.
Wounded.
Damn right,
I'm mean,
bitter,
inflamed.
Scars are consistent
with battle.
Our conversations,
one continuous stream;
have beat
the life out of me.
The nice out of me.
Ragged are my edges.
My metamorphosis,
I wear too proudly
For everyone to see.
What you've done to me,
What you've done to me.
Pretty words,
do not
decorate my
soul.

Broken

by Gereg Jones Muller

When you broke the little sake cup
while cleaning it, you wouldn't
let it go. Throw it away,
I said. It's done, it's
nothing. It served its purpose
nobly, and now it's done.

But you insisted, and at length
the cup returned, glued carefully together
by your father's craft. Still,
there remained the least of chinks where
the light shone through a thin spot,
and yes, when tried, there was still
the tiniest of leaks.

My friend, my dear,
there are things broken long
before the damage is known,
And sometimes, sometimes,
not the truest bond in all the worlds
can make perfect the thing
that's been broken.

Who Will Be There

by Aubrie Anne

What cruel wind tears us apart?
When hands can no longer be used as canes,
We are sure to fall.
Not on stones, but on layers of separation.
And who's to care when we're alone?
And when the wind bellows,
False whispers in its wake,
Who will be there to comfort us?

All That Finds Me Gone

by Brian Frederick

Don't worry your pretty little face Katie Marie
this world doesn't intend you any harm.
I know the nights they find you cold
I've seen the emptiness inside your haunted eyes.
At least I have in my dreams.

May you never see just how vicious
the war it could become.
Here's to hope that you never need to know
the truth, the stories we could tell.
My love may not be visible,
but that doesn't mean that it's not there.

Dry those pain-filled tears Katie Marie,
This old man did not intend you any harm.
I know the lies they have told,
I've felt the anger inside your wounded heart,
I lived that life in my nightmares.

May you never see just how vicious
the war it could become.
Here's to hope that you never need to know
the truth, the stories we could tell.
My love may not be visible,
but that doesn't mean that it's not there.

Maybe one day when you wake up,
you'll see all that finds me gone.
Every lost day will suddenly make sense.
The thing that's always been missing,
was in the cold, dark shadows all along.
Somewhere inside I really feel
that missing me was the most spectacular gift
I ever could have given to you.

Just walk on by Katie Marie,
This big beautiful world is yours to own
I know the stars they shine for you.
I've seen future inside your wondrous eyes.
At least I have in my dreams.

Edinburgh

by Nicole Bailey

Leaves fall heavy to the floor
shadows move over
a vacant parking lot.
A pay phone rings for no one.

My solitude is always
a world away from yours.

Quintessence of knowable objects
familiar things with familiar names,
but when I look at you I can't recall
what we're calling ourselves these days.

My solitude speaks volumes.

A fog rolls sideways
in our collective lives,
the force of our bad habits
setting us apart.

Pacific, Atlantic
the airless Dead Sea,
would you feel it if these things
were between us?

My solitude is always
a world away from yours.

II.

we of wellspring, we of weed

I Love It Best

by Catherine Frazer

I love it best on
Days when life
Seizes us and
Shakes the pride
Out of us like so
Many fallen leaves
Tossed about on
Crisp rustling storms
Flung against us
Like the Days of
Our Lives Autumn
Sweeps amber and
Gold in abandon finally
Covering the ground
In careless piles

THE PEACH

by Jerriann Law

The peach was soft fuzz rubbed across the cheek

The scent inhaled: a ripeness of peach sweetness

With eyes held closed, the peach itself was my entire world

I lived inside the peach while the peach was my circumference, my outreach

A projection of me for others to see and feel

Touch me know my soft allure, feel me, taste me, and eat me

Savor me as the dearest peach you'll ever meet

Inside my red flesh beats a peach seed heart

This heart is beating a tempo fleet-

Fast-quickening...smooth, true

Song of hushed amore

You, close, close, come closer, closer

You lean in and listen: sniff, sniff, sniff

Scent of peach, taste the peach juice ripe upon the tongue

Swallow...swallow...follow...falling into waiting arms wanting only to love

Rock Canyon

by Linda N. Chaston

I drove almost to the clouds today
They hung, heavy and dark
Obscuring the familiar crags and peaks
I stood under their blanketing shelter
And felt I might reach out my hand
To touch their hem.
Rainy days of childhood recalled
Snug in self-made sanctuary
Boxes and chairs and sofa cushions
Secure under a woolly roof.
Hours of adventure and fantasy
Shadowy and safe in my corner of a bigger world
Today I reached my hand toward the darkening down
And felt that way again.

Morning Sea Walk

by Shari Rood

As I walked out this morning the smell of salty air
filled my lungs

The sun was just starting to rise, and a heavy mist was
still clinging to the houses along the row

I stepped barefoot on to the finely cut grass lawn in
order to make my way to the road

The grass was slippery and cool and I jumped over the
crushed oyster shells that bordered the edge of the
lawn

The pavement felt good and solid beneath my feet

I looked up to see the mist dispersing and the sun
starting to warm the tops of the houses

The trees were glimmering with dew spatters and the
refracted light danced and shot color in all directions

I could hear the ocean now

The incessant pounding of surf on sand

It was muffled by the houses and the road but I had
crossed the street and could just make out the sand
dunes ahead

The sprinklers on the corner were already on

The hissing caught my attention and I looked to see
a garden of English roses and larkspur, hollyhock and
lavender

I was now starting to reach the path of sand that would
lead me past the house and over the hill to the sea

The sand was damp between my toes and I hurled my
half asleep body up the hill

At the top of the hill the ocean and horizon stretched
out before me as though no one but me had ever seen it

The waves were lazy this morning and curling and
jumping and sliding across the sand and retreating
again

The sky was a pale robin's egg blue

The sun had not risen far enough in the sky to
illuminate the dark sea

Further out the water looked moody and was the
color of ash

I turned to the left and walked away from the town
and the houses, a lone jogger ran past with a nod

As I walked, the sun began to spread light across the
waves making the caps look white

I saw dolphin fins, gray and sliding through the water
without a sound

They must be fishing, I thought. I saw them begin to
circle and leap

I heard the seagulls crying from above, waiting for
some bits of torn flesh to rise to surface

Further along the beach, I saw a dead turtle, it was a
massive thing

It was bloated and bobbing like a cork in the shallow
part of the water

I stood and watched for a long time, the sea moved its
body in such a way that I thought it was alive

It finally washed up on shore and I saw that its eyes
were gone

I continued up the beach, the sand now glittering like
tiny jewels

I walked on and now the sun was squarely in
the center of the sky

I saw people setting up camp with chairs and coolers
and umbrellas

Children were starting to busy themselves with the
work of building sandcastles

I could spot the shell collectors because they walked
with their heads down

I finally reached the marker, an old watch tower that
was used during World War II

It was just a turret, really, with stairs and a small room
at the top

The glass was long gone and the stone was weathered
and forgotten

I touched the hard rock and turned back

Solitude

by Cheri Scutti

Mountain top solitude.
I look around, I see sky, clouds & trees.
I hear the wind, I feel it on my face.
A brisk shiver down my back.
And I'm alone.

A hawk flies overhead.
He coasts effortlessly.
Circling through the sky.
Looking down for prey.

The trees moan as the wind bends their limbs.
The final fall leaves blow away.
I hear their dry, scratching sounds as they skip across
the ground.

The clouds move and transform into playful shapes.
The sun tries to peak through and warm my face.

No one else around, just me.
Then, I see the outline of someone coming my way.
They change their course and fade away.

Never close enough to touch.
My heart aches like the bending trees in the wind.
Longing for a warm soft place to melt.

There is an echo inside my chest.
A void forbidden to be filled.
An emptiness for all time.

Secret Garden

by Mark Bradshaw

The garden, long deserted
Had returned to natures care
It's beauty now breathtaking
No other could compare

The lawns were trimmed off neatly
By the wild deer that now roamed
The wind then took the dead leaves
It looked like they'd been combed

The stream had made it's own path
Through mossy coated rocks
Bursts of colour sprang out
From marigolds and flocks

Once sparsely planted daffodils
Had spread to carpet gold
The oak tree in the centre
Stood majestic, tall and bold

Now huge imposing gunnera
Had formed a passage deep
Whilst the willow by the lake
Continued still to weep

This natural growing paradise
Mocked gardeners and their toil
The plants here need no pruning
Just sun and rain and soil

Unnatural Forces

by Aubrie Anne

The riverbed, floored by sand and rocks, was forever changing
The water was always in motion, pushing the bed in a constant direction
Trees emerged from the ground and drank from the springs below
The water from the river fed them, providing it's roots with life
No one seemed to notice the painting of the leaves, natural kaleidoscopes
Or the changing levels in the water, a steady rise and fall
Rain would strike the surface, leaving its mark on the facade
The source regenerated and was flawless once again
Wind would blow, but it would only skip along the surface
Nothing could stop the river, not even a rock could delay it for long

Then men came
They built their walls

The river is damned

Now, stagnant and foul is the liquid
Backed up with disease and dying foliage
No animal dare drink for fear of wilting
Like the plants who lack the ability to flee

There is no pulse or slow beating waves
Against the barren and lonely shores
The fish will not spawn this year
They mourn their loss in silence
This is now a place that lacks the strength
To fight back against unnatural forces

Hydrophobia

by John S. DeStefano Jr.

The ocean lapped the luscious shore
slowly inching its way up the sand
This treasure we had traveled to admire
    now was pushing us away
    like an overanxious dog
    jumping all over our Sunday best
Still we saw only its shiny sheen silver surface
    hiding its currents and malevolent intentions
We heard the roar of the surf up the beach
And imagined our homes immersed in the deep sea
    immortal blue shadow
Yet nature's flooding force smiled upon us
Inviting us into her cool, salty rhythm
We stoned her
    destroyed her alluring glass coating
And we ran barefoot along the golden beach
    laughing.

Rain

By Karl Edward Lee

The impenetrable grey
Horizon, occluding
The proverbial drop of ink.

So it remains

And so, steadfast
In your resolute pose
Righteous rigor rises within
The core of your being
If you were not right
What would you be?

Lost, In grey
In wilderness, Seeking
Foundation
Lost before
So long ago.

I saw you reach
Within, to pull
Yourself from that
Which would claim you.
I did not have to act.
I waited.
For the rain to pass.

A Haunting Moon

by Bert Bell

Walking alone beneath the Pierrot moon,
I see its geisha face above the trees,
And try to whistle some forgotten tune,
I smell the blossoms in the gentle breeze.

Soft clouds of cotton slowly move across
The ashen face of that celestial mime,
Reminding me of good friends I have lost;
I come upon the hill we used to climb.

Sadly, the moon looks like Marcel Marceau,
Though memories obliterate my view;
Without you here the moon has lost its glow.
My love, my life is just a void without you.

Sway

by Melanie Bertenshaw

I watch the branches sway in the wind.
Never broken... only allowing to bend.
I take in this lesson with vigor,
forgetting a tree is not human

Je Vois Tout

by Vicki F. Chavis

A fast walk, no time to spare,
a lace wrap seductively
flutters down a breeze
and I catch her, right there
under the green awning
on the corner of Rue Mayron
and Rochambeau
bending over wild roses
in someone's city garden,
bricked-in completely,
bordered by fumes
and you would think,
"She's here for a reason."
Not a drop of blood pools
from the thorn in her thumb,
how would a ghost bleed,
anyway? The city presses in
on her sideways in hard bursts
of blue-green exhaust
and the sounds of too many boots
stomping past to concentrate.
Her hands flail through the vines,
committing no sin, attending only
to a frail flush of beauty, the whispering
of another spring. Suddenly distracted,
her eyes dart, turning to slits in the sun.
When she sees me, I have already
been watching at length and she

mouths the words right there
in the middle of Paris,
"I'm having trouble with words."
Considering a move to
the country; lavender and sunflower
fields on her mind, she can't
remember the words anymore
for love, apple, look.

Beatrice

by Catherine Bourne

"Would you like one lump, or two?"
That was the first question my grandma would ask
as I sat down for tea
during our monthly visits in her little cottage
between the sea and the cypress trees.

She lived right on the cliff along the Pacific Ocean,
overlooking the white sandy shores,
where the surfers could always be seen during an afternoon swell.
"And a little milk too, grandma,"
I would add, with anticipation.

She used her best china
brought back from England;
blue and white landscapes from Churchill
stamped 'Willow' underneath.

The plates were piled high with assorted treats:
Marshmallow pinwheel cookies, little biscuits for dipping.
raspberry filled shortbreads, and apple pie.

The smell of sweet pastries and seasoned teas
filled the room like a warm hug.
We could only smile.
I always left with a bellyache.
But, oh, how I loved this time we shared,
talking about everything we could,
at a table set for two.

My divorce came swiftly,
shortly after her passing
and both left a void
that I found unable to fill.

We were a new family of three:
myself,
my daughter
and my son.

Everything had changed
and we lacked the stability and communication
one needs
to remain confident and sure
in troubled times.

We had to move
and the kids changed schools,
leaving behind friends and any familiar routine.
I felt us
slowly slipping
into three separate lives
without ever sharing our thoughts or feelings.

"Mom, I miss great grandma,"
My son said, one afternoon.
"So do I..."
I said, holding back my tears.
We hugged,
but
that was all.

We had lost our way,
forgetting
we still had each other.

That night,
alone I cried
until a distant thought took shape;
tomorrow would be different.

When the kids came home from school
they were greeted
by surprise.

I had put out our best china.
My grandma brought it back
all the way from England;
blue and white landscapes from Churchill
stamped 'Willow' underneath.

The plates were piled high with assorted treats:
Marshmallow pinwheel cookies, little biscuits for dipping,
raspberry filled shortbreads, and apple pie.

The smell of sweet pastries and seasoned teas
filled the room like a warm hug.
We could only smile.
"Would you like one lump, or two?"
I asked, with anticipation.
We talked about everything we could,
at a table set for three.

And now,
when I feel the world tugging at us
in three different directions,
this is how we come back together,
never forgetting that we always have each other.

III

we of weapon, we of web

Buttercup

by Heige Boehm

You are there I am nowhere; windows all around.
Tokens of affection collecting dust; stones lay on the ground.
Photos fading, news on radio, war brewing in men's heart.

First day of summer, plants growing, are there happy times to come?
Slippery thoughts crashing, stay unscathed, will never happen.
A new child will be born, jubilee; mud dried up blowing in your eye.
I wanted him so dear, beat the life into me; finger nails chewed right to pain.

Every line a song tap, tap; cut my head right off.
Wedding dress filled with pie; soiled with old; possibility with ink.
Turn around, shake with fear, women all had dreams, taken blood, memorial, no one will forget.
Create a web, spin, capture yourself, can you get out?
Screams, night time rests in evil.

There is no god, second hand information, so is mine; water puddles filled with laughter.
Global bullshit, Top Dog what a joke, do you think your own reality?
Save your seeds, stay awake, they will come.
Yellow school bus strapped in, taught with fear, sick minds doing, recoil, listen without your ears.

Dancing, free movement, beating hearts, back to
truth, we are not modern, dress in adornment, spikes
in your heals.
Sex on every wave of thought, explosion of your brain,
conform to the tired norm; fuck head!

Buttercups, remember? Tea leaves read by the witch
doctor, hang her by her head, or burn her while alive!
Superstition in wallet, it is my doing, for your bloated
stomach; so you eat rats and drink mud.

I live like a queen, come and you cannot have it. How
about a mosquito net?
Do you have flowers in your heart? Do you live in a
hut? Do you drink blood? If you are different to my
eye, should you want the same?

People are on their fat ass, give me more pizza! Make
a sad story; I have wounds, look what they did, I..........
Remember your passion for love, or did you eat your
possibility?

Rage in all, suck it up, stay afloat, pull the muck over
your eyes, leave the shit on your step, go back to bed,
plant a tree for those unthought.
Suffer for what we do not have, bleed for what we
keep, divide our hearts, and take from all, so they can
have, so they can charge, and I can pay, and you can die!

Are we not they?

Dark Moon Child

by Josafat

I raise you up,
in dreams,
above my head.
The circle of your face, pearly white,
bears eyes that like flames reveal
smokeless fires that seem to steal
from lofty windows their tinted light.

I offer you up,
with hope,
sweet sacrifice.

Upon the world's altar of judgment,
I lay you down in untimely repose,
as your tiny hands open and close
to catch my tears of bitter ointment.

I give you up,
decided,
my vein, my heart.

Hidden from others' frenzied fury,
your blood, my blood, alone I spill,
as my womb burns in feverish guilt,
releasing its flood of crimson beauty.

I grieve you,
cowardly,
under a tolerant dark moon.

Private Jones Reality

by A.W. Hazzard, Jr.

Hey there! Is it real now?
Fuck was it real then?
Rain coming down.
Babies cryin'
Hot,
Wet,
Brothers dyin'.

Guts hanging out somewhere.
Smoke rising from the jungle.
Rats feasting on their death.

Sitting on my bunker,
Sitting next to a hero.
Junk in his head.
Lying on his bed
Wishing to be home instead.

Starlight, Star bright,
Victor Charlie's visiting us tonight.

Wire 's strung-
water buffalo's dung.
Ballads sung- Death's sure to come.

Fuck! Maybe it will be real then.
Nobody knows when!

Viet Nam. Twilight Zone.
Acid, Mary Jane, Barb's and Speed
All for a few M.P.C.
What was real when?
Smoke rising from my mouth.
Jimmy Hendrix Playing "Strange Things."

It doesn't matter anymore;
Be she lady or be she whore.
It doesn't matter any more.
Pvt. Jones is dead!
It doesn't matter any fucking more.
Not to Pvt. Jones at the morgue.

Poison

by Sarah Rudderham-Baldwin

Drink the poison, to ease the pain.
The poison that slips through the lips
And the veins
Morphing my judgement
Clouding my mind.
Troubles are faded
And worries are blind.

Slip out of life and into another
Live for tonight.
Tomorrow will suffer.

Welcome Aphrodite

by Paul J. Mackintosh

The anticipation is transitory
Nervously waiting
Gnawing at Bacchanalian nails
Yet with an indulgent Claret smile
And needy eyes flicking surreptitiously
Across wild nubile landscapes

She hears the random humming
A generator of fickle power she knows
Peak intensity then nothing soon
But for now the vinous airs
Rancid and redolent
Cost misty-eyed Liber his sanity

Leap as dark chords riff and luff
The veils and foolish pastel skirts
Of tempting maidens
That dart with squeals of soprano glee
She watches from crimson wings
Awaiting the cue from Bacchus' lips

The rheumy eyes of drunken Gods
Feather rainbow blurs and turning silk
Take time to mark the evening sun
That lights the fringe of gibbous flesh within
But once this child of breaking waves is seen
Young Bacchus is imprisoned by rapturous lust

She places her soft young heart in his tender hands
Where once she dreamed of sea foam and
pomegranates
Now hot white fingers of intensity wrap a flaming grip
Around her waist, and pull her into the inferno
For on this eve of Thalia's graceful conception
The epitome of earthly love is unleashed upon this
feast

My Metaphor

by Sarah Rudderham-Baldwin

I am my weak and broken smile.

I am that dark and distant isle.

I am the love that fills my heart.

I am the finish and the start.

I am my siblings growing old.

I am the stories I was told.

I am the scars carved in my skin.

I am your secrets deep within.

I am the final tear I cry.

I am the questions asking why.

I am the doubt that's in your eyes.

I am the moment my life dies.

I am the last breath I will take.

I am that life-ending mistake.

Of Fire and Home

by Connor Mooney-Collett

My life needs not dreaming,
For my very existence is a delusion,
I have no memory of my years gone past,
Thick smoke clouding my foresight,
From my burning home I am trapped in,
I will never escape,
Nor will my family.

Orphaned

by Janet Renee Cryer

As we walk into the hotel room, three boys, the coach and myself, I knew danger is ahead. It was something that I had warning due to my intuition but never knew why. The town seemed pleasant enough for a swim meet but the town was hiding something. Something was amiss and yet could not be pointed out or pin to one such thing. He is watching but could never be seen. Was he in the hotel we were staying in or the restaurant we frequented during our stay, it is unknown and so familiar at the same time. His eyes crept over me time and time again. I felt every inch of my body tremble in fear and the others thought I was losing my mind. Was I losing my mind, a 13 year old girl going to a swim meet with the coach and three boys? I might have been but I was the best swimmer on the team and they were not going to let me go so easily.

What is a bit of insanity?

He is still staring and leering, I feel like he can see right through me and though he is a stranger, he feels so familiar. I am scared and the boys look at me, once again, like I am paranoid. Am I paranoid or is the stranger leering upon me waiting for a chance to pounce? The coach is gone to register us for the meet since we arrived a day later than expected. I am scared and the scariest thing is if I am gone, will I be missed? I am orphaned, some say by choice others say by insanity... I fear if I am missing I will not be missed.

Have I orphaned myself by circumstance or by insanity, it is unknown for sure, will I by missed?

I walk into my room and it is empty. The boys are in the other room, I can hear them. They are having a great deal of fun, it is beyond any fun I have ever experience in my childhood. My life is about work, school, and swimming. Fun is not an option. I am stuck in my room and it feels like the years have passed. I will not look in a mirror as I am afraid of who will look back. I know he is still lurking out there and the boys have become quiet. Are they still there? I try the door between our rooms and it will not open. I am pounding and all I hear is laughter but I don't think they hear me pounding. Why do they sound so much older than a minute ago when I left their room? Is the coach back?

Help, I do not think they notice I am not there.

A piercing sound enters my room and yet my door does not open. There is a burn that I feel and I can not see where it has come from. Have I been shot? The man is still out there, as he shot me? I can not tell, I feel the burn but it looks like a mere prick of a needle not a bullet wound as I had imagined. Things are getting fuzzy, where am I? I am still in the hotel room that the boys, coach, and I arrived at. I can barely move, why is this? I know the man is still out there, I feel him leering at me still.

Will he ever go away.
Bright lights, burning eyes, I can not see in the mirror. I knew it would be scary to look but made a slight attempt. It hurts too bad, I will stop looking. The lights are dimming. I feel like I am trapped and even though the man is still watching me, I can not get away. I can not see him and yet I feel as though I have been tied down. I can not move my arms, only my legs and they feel extremely heavy. My legs are no longer moving, why is this? I am inside my hotel room and yet I can not move. No one is here and the boys are playing in the other room. Why can no one hear my screams for help? I feel as though I am drowning in the sound of my voice.

It darkens.

The room is still empty and dark but I can not sleep. I am bound to the room and feel as though I will never be able to move. It has been so long if it is dark, why haven't the boys checked on me? It has been hours, days, and even feels like years and yet I feel no hunger just want to be able to move, be heard, and be missed.

I am not missed, I am orphaned, and no one cares. I will go to sleep now.

Moments Slip Away

by Nancy R. Hatch

Treasured photos fill
time-worn antique ladder shelves
with no space to spare

Ghosts from the past, so
easily resurrected,
crumble back to dust

Life's treasured moments:
bite-size morsels melting as
soon as they appear

How do we account
for the time we've spent chasing
restless empty dreams?

Green Monsters

by William E. Hampton

When asked for the secret of hitting
Babe Ruth said, Y a gotta know your onions,
Wee Willie Keeler said, "Hit'em where they ain't,"
Ted Williams said, G et a good ball to hit,

Ty Cobb said, F uck you.

The picture hangs on my wall, filled with intent
Ty Cobb sliding into Jimmy Austin's shins at third
The dirt spewing up in agony, as the Georgia Peach's spikes
Slice through more than the basepath.

It was a time of madmen and green monsters, when Cobb knew Navin
When the summer sun cut through the savage symmetry of the infield
Like quicksand, ready to swallow you up just for standing still
When the stench of stubborn glory was carried up by the urgent dust
And the roar of the crowd was a roar for blood.

Here in the shadow of Navin field that became Briggs and then Tiger Stadium
Now as empty as Cobb's grave, crying out for its madmen
That picture carries the hate spit through Ty Cobb's

gritted teeth
Hate spit not at Austin, but to the world in general, to life, to me.

At the end of his career, when asked if he had any regrets
Cobb simply said that he wished he had made more friends
As if what finally haunted him was the missing memories
Of friends sacrificed to green monsters and the glory of the next base.

Time

by Raven Wilkie

Tick, tock
the universal clock ...
peeling off
years that mock.

Chained and fettered ...
with keyless lock.
And "time" stands laughing
at our foolish shock.

Ranting and raving
avails us naught ...
In its grasp
we are securely caught.

Merciless and cold,
it will have its way ...
with you, with me,
till our dying day.

Helpless we are,
to its savage rape ...
with bystanders standing,
mouths all agape.

Useless ones of
no substance, or shape ...
placidly waiting,
till it's them that it takes.

The strength I possessed
has become undone ...
now I just open my legs,
and admit that its WON!

Seams from In Between

by Karl Edward Lee

seams

Fragments of life
Parts Pieces Dreams
The fundamental fabrics that fit
In between the seams
The elusive precipice
Once gained
Awash now in perspective
Look around
More ledges to climb
Perhaps trust and love is enough
Enough to recover from the fall
The inevitable leap of faith
All the Kings men
Are merely parts themselves
Do you trust yourself enough
To recover
the fragments of your life
After you survey the carnage
After the crash
sitting in the aftermath
Perplexed
Wondering about the seams.

Ambivalent Existence

by Glenn Jr. Marchand

I have lived as a shadow;
Destined for political battle.
I have lived as a shadow;
Searching unto death for identity.
I have lived in a cave.
I am more than an ex-slave.
I am spirit; I am a divine entity.
I have lived as a shadow:
Battered, bruised and addled.
I have lived as a shadow.
I am invisible ability.
I am without serenity.

Ugly Ways

by Catherine Bourne

I'd like to say I love you
But I don't,
I'd rather die
And just those words burn a hole in my throat,
When I try
To choke them out.

Fact is
The negative thoughts
You've etched in my soul
Run deep throughout,
Creating one black hole.

I'm empty
Pained
Black-veined
Over-blamed
Forever chained in your daunting game.

Remember the night you told me about him?
He beat you,
He raped you,
He lied through his grin?

"He was crazy!" You said,
"Born Cherokee, one-half breed."
Mixed tones of voice you bled to me
Cut straight to my reality;
You hate a man who is part of me.

You see,
I remember when he finally left
After that day,
We both died a death
And while you kept on breathing,
I lay without breath.

Do I look like him?
Is it the nose on my face?
When you see me,
Do I take you to that old familiar place?
The one you recall,
Having his stinky breath in your face.

You retrace the pain he left in you,
In my face.
I can tell by the one time
You looked in my eyes,
You're reminded of him
Telling you all of his lies.

The, "I won't drink no more,
Or beat you
Or berate you
Or fuck those other whores",
Just one room over,
Behind closed doors.

Yeah, all those lies
I'm sure he bored you
With his half ass tries.
But now I must ask you,
I have so many 'whys'.

If I could see it in your face,
Why couldn't you see it in his eyes?
I'm so angry that you couldn't have become
More wise.

All I remember
Are your tears and your cries
But never doing nothing
As he caressed another's thighs,
In the room next door to mine.

While we heard,
Me, too young to realize
How absurd
You must have been
Just to stay and listen;

"It's that, Mary Cooper! How can it be?"
You cried,
"She's even in my class!"

Well you're sadly mistaken Mother
Because the both of you
Are certainly taking it in the ass
And if you weren't acting so weak,
I wouldn't be talking so crass!

But how could I make you understand?
I stare at my fingers
Wiggling nervous in my hands,
And count out loud
For each year I stand.

One, two, three, four and five,
I whisper to God,
For he knows I'm alive,

As I lay me down to sleep
I pray the Lord
My Mother I keep
'Cos daddy won't be here for long
It's dark, and I don't feel very strong.

I know the pattern
Like dot to dot
Like a robot, I trace the stars
With my finger in the air
It's better then watching my Mother stare
Through the muted light of the moon
Which cast through our window
Allowing me
A visual gloom.

It's suddenly so quiet and cold
And I feel so bare
Though dressed head to toe
In feety p.j.'s
At five years old,
I learned life's ***ugly ways.***

Spirits of Memory

by Shah Warton

Denial....
Spirits sneak quietly up our sleeves,
to exit through our eyes.
Then eye-to-eye we do deceive,
with tiny timid lies.

....Acceptance

When dire recollections,
start dripping from our lips,
tormented introspection,
will leave those spirits stripped.

DEATH

by Richard Soloway

I am waiting for Death to come,
but aren't we all, just waiting for that last visit?
Sometimes
I think of rushing to meet him, not in the way
you rush to a lover's arms, full of eager
anticipation and joy, but in the way
you go to the dentist or visit the
headmaster's study, wanting to get over
the inevitable. I have checked about a
visit to Switzerland because I am old and worn
out. My children need my money
more than I do and I don't want to linger on,
rotting piecemeal a hollow cadaver, still eating
and taking up space, no CPU functions left, just a
walking corpse. It seems wrong to go by one's
own hand and my dogs need me, but what is
the point? The world has too many old
people, who cares about one
more, or less? So I wait, he will come
soon, it would have been nice
To write just one thing that was
any good first.

The Reading

by Vicki F. Chavis

You walked into the psychic's den
with your plans and your dreams
stacked neatly like little red bricks
held together with the glue of reverence.

She reached round and plucked some truths
from your effluvia, spilled them out like glitter
on the table - carved in hypnotic cadences,
she was on a mission to entice.

Dripping ancient placebos into your veins,
she dragged me (the mother) into it - all those
past lives, my watery demise.
What could you say about my Titanic?

All you remember is her
tinkling laugh, her little joke
and the strong scent of sandalwood
tantalizing you all the way home.

IV.

we of welded, we of wealth

Eternal

by Tamera Bourne

My back against the trunk,
I observe the musicians
adjusting the instruments,
their slow progression of tuning
is like the first steps of fawn in late May.

The cords swirl into my mind like maple seeds in the wind.
Two seeds progress in the same current like a
couple fox-trotting across the open dance floor
to the bowing of the fiddle.

Each strum of the guitar
speeds their dance into a meringue
taking me back to a Costa Rican open-air
bar at twilight on a June evening.

Each beat of the drum reminds
me of the Lakota dancing
for a successful buffalo hunt.

As the harmonies blend,
I see people of all cultures
lying on the grass at a summer picnic,
talking, laughing, playing together.

Dreamers

by Richard Soloway

Who are we, that write and strut and pose,
Sometimes a verse of gold, hidden in the prose?
We deal in dreams, reality is made of smoke,
we hear
insubstantial reverberations of lost chords, and
diminished echoes of the howling of wolves. The
tinkle of cow bells and the lowing of the cattle
merge
with the bell-bird's song and the sky lark ascending
as it
trills its territorial way to heaven. Reality is a mirage,
all is
'maya', and through the false solidity of the
temporal materialism of the day we try to
reach a metaphysical truth that
others might call a tissue of lies.
We are the dreamers, the useless of the world, at
school we lost ourselves staring out of the window,
while
Euclid and Archimedes proved something to do
with the square on the hypotenuse, or
perhaps the volume of water that an old man's body
displaces. We floated
with our muse, and saw the three graces. Do we
live in the illusion of the flesh and the world
when we

spin gossamer filaments of unreality? Or do we
search for truth and then seek to escape the pain
of that vision in the bottle, and lose ourselves
in filigrees of smoke
and perfumed flesh? How can our lovers
and partners trust us
when fact is fiction
and fiction is mythology. Others say
they do not declare undying love, except
when they mean it to be eternal. Seducers say
they love whoever they are with just to get
them into carnal sin, but we say that
we love each and every one that we meet, for
we do, but time for us is not eternal, love is
transitory but heartfelt. We feel the
emotions of the world, and all the
pain and all the glory. We are
empaths through and through and
wear our souls on our shirts and
our hearts skewered on the barbecue.

Apple Picking

by Lindsay Black

He says he wants to go apple picking,
a romantic afternoon, just the two of us.
What he actually means
is he'd like to go somewhere
where apples grow,
which means trees,
which means woods, and shade and
secluded sunlight-dappled clearings
in the woods where, maybe,
we'll find ourselves alone.
Where, maybe, I'll let him kiss me.
Just a little, maybe.
Maybe he'll kiss so well
I'll let him back me up against a tree
and kiss me more, a little.
Wrap my arms around his neck and taste
the sandwiches we shared for lunch.
Lift my dress, a little.
Test the softness of unmown grass and
fallen leaves beneath my back.
Maybe, just a little.
I tell him I would love
to go apple picking.

Three generations.

by Richard Archer

Daughter mother and granddaughter,
A holy trinity for the Ipod generation,
Get on the bus every working day,
And sit in their usual pattern.
The daughter with her bleached hair,
Held back in a face lift tight bun,
Has the best fake tan a bottle can give,
And never puts down her mobile phone.
The mother young and also bottle tanned,
With her fake fur hood always up,
Sits next to her daughter in silence,
Never acknowledging she's there.
Grandmother with her roots showing,
Dressed in granddaughter's cast offs,
Proudly defies you it seems to guess her age
As she smiles and cracks her make up.

Catch Sunlight

by Gereg Jones Muller

I love you more than words begin to say,
for all the words I've uttered on the theme.
For words are history, while love's today.

However clever, words are shadow-play
cast on a cavern wall: a myth, a dream.
I love you more than words begin to say.

Simplicity's an art, a part I play,
as truthful as the cat refusing cream.
For words are history, while love's today.

Still, subtlety was silenced yesterday:
sincerity saw through wit's cunning scheme.
I love you more than words begin to say.

Why, even now, embracing you, I pray
for rhymes: as soon catch sunlight on the stream.
For words are history, while love's today.

I hold you close and cast all art away,
compelling though my muse's urge may seem:
for words are history, while love's today.
I love you more than words begin to say.

Reading

by Amelia Brueggemann

Give me words
that flit and flutter
and fall
under my tongue
and write me
off

Incredulous
yet believable
as an inept
deliverer of
the unspoken
word

Fine tips of fingers
fumble with
the need for
crisp and fine
edges

The smell of
new or old
like
money well
spent

He Doesn t Understand

by E. Louise Osburn

She was packing her suitcase
When he came in.
She said she was tired of the fussing and din.
He stood there lost
In thought for a minute.
Then he grabbed a suitcase
And started putting clothes in it.
"What are you doing?"
"I'm tired of fussing, too,
So I'm packing my suitcase.
I'm going with you."

Healing

by Lindsay Black

I will be the vessel and carry health
to all the broken souls.
I will take the shards and
chew them to sand for castles and
stick-written messages that
wash away but made you smile.
I will carry your hurt in the pocket in
my chest; I fill the pouch with
your tears and desires.
There is no healing until the
splinter is removed.
I use them to pin my dress
up around my knees so I can
jump the chasm where the
nightmares hide.
Yours will be dropped among them.
They will wake me early
to get on with the work
I do alone.

Postcards from America

by Nicole Bailey

the waitress drips forward
unstable on aged legs
and turns a deaf ear to my order.
(she'll bring black coffee anyway)

woman behind the counter
grins delight to see her son
she makes introductions
as he leans on the bar
looking wasted and stoned.
(when they stand side by side,
mother and son,
it's hard to tell which one
is older)

the waitress brings black coffee
and it shakes as she sets it down
going off to scrub a table raw.
(will I, one day, wear round cakes of rouge
and lipstick that speaks of
crusted ketchup?
will I think myself beautiful
when even the old drunks
have stopped calling me so?)

woman behind the counter
she whispers to her son
encouraging mother's whispers,
her penciled eyebrows confer close together

and she hands him her tips from the day.
(enough for a pack of cigarettes
and a sealed bottle of Jack)

the old men crowd the bar stools
eat nothing, drink water,
leering at the young girls
just returned from a night of dancing.
(their skin glitters surreal with sweat
their smiles luminescent in neon).

a man behind me trades stocks
on his brand new cellular phone
running business from across town,
he worries, commands and fidgets
out on a date with his wife.

woman behind the counter,
she's never left the state,
but a customer once told her
Florence is nice in fall.

this woman behind the counter
she may look a bit worse for wear
but she has a wisdom
my travel-worn shoes won't find.

the waitress won't be around for long
you can hear her creaking from the kitchen
but when she's gone the old men will know it
and raise a black coffee to Maude.

a man behind me flips his cell phone shut
and his voice turns to a smile,
as he holds the fork to his wife's lips
because she can't lift it anymore.

Touch

by BurningIvy

Soft on contact.
Shirt, wrinkles like leaf veins
feels warm on flesh and scratches bone.
Rippled, wet like the sweat on a blade of grass.
Skin, rough on eyelids
covers myself, wrapped in this unlikely layer.
Hair, sounds like a violinist's song
blanketing my thoughts.
Passion is to touch
and feel.
Moving in rhythm and swaying in rhyme
are tears on cheek.
Dancing on your deaf fingertips is sensory.
Fingers see.
My hands lean close to hear you move against me.
Nails taste your skin,
it stings the tongue and leaves her
begging, aching for more.
Toes on ankles squirm against.
Protesting regions must conform.
Ambiguous.
How do I describe the touch of yours that moves me so well?
I see touch like smell and smell is sound and sound is taste and taste is sight.
To touch is to love.
When loving becomes more than that of the eyes you can taste it.

Bitter sound is sweet when helping hands race to aid.
Oh love, I can taste you.
Soft and sweeping,
skin on bone,
love on love,
let us lie.
Sweetly sings our song does touch.
We do touch even when apart are we.
Never minding our idle doubts and insecurities
we drink of each others flaws
wishing never to change and
you and I are each other.
What you feel, I touch and also become.
Blind, I could still see you.
How does one hear but to first have listened and
embraced?
And we do embrace, we hold each other in our gaze.
Your scent paralyzes motion.
I can smell you love.
Sweet savors pleasing to my legs against yours.
My arms are wrapped in your blanket.
Take me so that I might touch.

Jewelry Box Dance

by Daniel E. Lodermeier

Without you my world stands still
    as I lay here in the dark.
I lay beside your treasured gifts
    and beside your golden heart.

The pictures that are held inside
    bring back the days of old.
They fade more with every year
    but memories don't grow cold.

My life slowly spins in circles
    though I go nowhere at all.
I just stay here in this box
    and wait for you to call.

The song which I'm dancing to
    only starts when you're around.
Just open up your jewelry box
    for that's where I am found.

I See You

by Paul J. Mackintosh

I see the light that suffered untold conscience pains
Illuminating sacred hearts, I see cold lips
That speak a prayer of fallacy and speak again
Whispering the words of submission with hate
And secret intentions
Defiance grew from that precious seed
Of wit and harsh realisation
You shone so bright, you glorious star, you favourite son
A tailless comet streaking across the void
Who dared to think, who dared to need
And against His furious wrath you raged
A challenge unlike any known
Speaking out against cruelty and domination
Cast down in flaming glory and blistering nobility
Our only hope in a careless world
Our shining light in the black
Ignoring false propaganda and pious hate
Reviving freedom and true choice
Against institutionalised terror
And mental suppression to arrogant conformity
I see you in the strong hearts of men
And in the tender arms of women
I see you in a passionate kiss
And between welcoming thighs
I see you in life's twinkling eye
And a moment lived for pleasure
I see you in tolerance
And true, life affirming love

I need to light the world

by Crystal Stone

I need an adrenaline **rush**.

I need to feel like I am living and not just sitting
around
wasting so much time and youth that should be in use.
I need to shatter the stars beneath my tree carved
treasures
while letting the shards rain all over my dance...

I need to feel **alive**.

I need to jump in puddles and get mud all over a pure
white dress fresh off my sewing machine while being
scolded for sticking my fingers in the cookie dough
my parents left on the table for baking another time.

I need to **move**.

I need to melt the ice that my feet have become and
let
the fear subside so I can be something more than still.
I need to flirt with the (cute) boy that I am head over
heels
for and just say something stupid that will stick in his
mind (forever).

I need to get **out** of my comfort zone.

I need to write (love) letters to someone who won't
ever read them
and dance ballet only to **fall on my face** at the feet

of a person
carrying roses for the lovely girl next to me and just laugh for
all of the serious people in the audience that were **holding it in**.

I need to **live**.

I need to let a scream pierce the silence just because I can
and praise (God) at a concert full of people dressed in black
that are screaming for other reasons than me...more than just
because they can but because they *can't* be who they want to be.

I need to do more than just sit here dreaming of what I could be
(I need to light the world.)

The Lap Dance

by Richard James

I look at your body,
Your casing so clean,
My hands they are shaking,
As I turn on your screen,

My system is loading,
I'm overflowing with joy,
I can't wait any longer,
To play with this toy,

You're wireless and lightweight,
And even compact,
I feel nervous and twitchy,
With you on my lap,

Then suddenly my God,
I'm all out of breath,
How could this happen?
The blue screen of death,

You betray me my love,
I'm really irate,
How could you do this?
You bastard Bill Gates!

In this world,
Nothing can beat,
Something so pure,
As CTRL-ALT-DELETE.

A Sheep in Wolf's Clothing

by Catherine Frazer

I wore you
On the edge
Wrapped around
Me like a sheep in
Wolf's clothing
My shoulder tucked
Under your arm
Tight my head
Cradled into your
Chest like a dove
Waiting for morning
As you sipped
Away my sadness
We watched the
Sun rise

Change of Heart

by Linda N. Chaston

Your kisses didn't stop my heart
Or leave me, weak-kneed and wilted,
Frantically scrambling for my dignity
While toppling headlong
For the millionth time

Never really a mystery man;
No hidden motives to twist my brain
Into a peace of mind train wreck
Emotional baggage bloodied and smeared
All over the place

Miraculous actually
That I noticed you at all --
Not exactly my M.O. at the time —
But there you were.

And every day
There you were

Steady and straight
Brutally honest
Unabashedly tender
Falling headlong, eyes wide open
Only for me

And those kisses now?
Breathless wonder!

Such A Sweet Fantasy

by Stan Cohen

Her hair, dark as summer's night
Flowing past those eyes, shining like stars
With that one glance, lasting for eternity, like sight of shooting star
My one wish, how in you it has come true

Those lips move so tender, like ocean's still rest
With each wave, a moment to treasure
Oh to be the moon, to compel those lips
Like lighthouse to ship, her radiance so attracts

What a splendour is her touch, such a treasure to my senses
Each so enticed, in awe of her allure
Such a wonder is her caress, like the breeze
With such light of grace, on most pleasant of sun filled eve's

I hear her body singing to me, the sweetest of serenades
Such humbling melodies this ear has heard, oh how these eyes admire
Drawn to those legs, formed so perfect
As if sculpted from the most passionate of desires

To hear her sigh, to make her moan
Such delights, I do so crave
Waking in her arms, I do so long
Life with her, oh what a dream

Father in Waiting

by Richard James

I sit up late,
Alone I wait,
My daughters birth,
A closer date.

I know I'll try,
To be the best,
Do what I know,
Figure out the rest.

I pray the world,
To her will be,
A kinder place,
Than it was to me.

I sit and talk,
My love distraught,
We discuss things,
We both weren't taught.

We calculate,
My love and I,
On colour of hair,
And colour of eye.

I grapple with fears,
My love in tears,
We saw this point,
Far off in years.

Fate takes no heed,
Of plans and schemes,
It changes plots,
And re-writes scenes.

Our river was blocked,
A new path was found,
Plunged in with my daughter,
Over uncovered ground.

I smile as I think,
Of all she could do,
But who will she look like,
Me or you?

Weight

by Amelia Brueggemann

These hands have held
and been held,
wrung by the
anguished
brushed by the lips
of the forged idealist
and folded
neatly in prayer

These arms have
cradled new life
wrapped the waists
of cured relationships,
been crossed to
shield, have carried
their weight.

This chest has
heaved, sustained
the fleck of blues and
broken vessels,
carried fleeting
creatures
donned with wings

These legs have
pressed on,
endured, wrapped
the body of another
have shaken
have been
weak

These eyes have
seen the press
of life, these ears
have muted the
heavy sighs, and
this body has
racked with
true, and genuine
joy

This body has
carried, bent and
broken beneath
the pressure
the torrent of
time, and has
sustained,
survived

www.ingramcontent.com/pod-product-compliance
Lightning Source LLC
Chambersburg PA
CBHW071612040426
42452CB00008B/1318

* 9 7 8 1 9 3 5 0 0 3 0 8 3 *